Coping
with the
Horroffice

How to tame your working day

Heena Pattni

A CIP record for this book is available from the British Library.

The moral right of Heena Pattni to be identified as the author of this work has been asserted.

Copy edited by Wendy Hobson

Edited by Deborah Taylor

Cover Design by Ajay Pattni

Author Photograph by Louise Young Photography

Published by Heena Pattni

Get a head start on Coping with your Horroffice now.

Get the *Ten Top Tips for Coping with the Horroffice*

and the **Awesomeness Tick List** at www.heenapattni.com.

Acknowledgements

I am normally pretty rubbish at saying thank you, especially when it's an important thank you. I get tongue tied and red-faced and the words get stuck. But in this case I have had the luxury of time and a keyboard to fine-tune the words, finesse the flow and put it all in print – I'm a lucky girl and am grabbing the opportunity with both hands.

There are a lot of people without whose well-meaning interference, gentle pushing and subtle shoving, this book would not have seen the light of day.

Vijay Pattni – thank you for constantly telling me I am wasting my time and talent when I am not writing. Thank you for nagging me every time I have strayed from my literary path and hounding me until I begin writing again. Thank you also for finding the time to read, review and feedback on this book, even when you apparently have a life of your own.

Ajay Pattni – thank you for always being such a huge fan of my work and reading my stuff even though you're not a fan of 'reading for pleasure'. And thank you for all the free website set-up, being my personal IT support department, and for co-creating the cover of Coping with the Horroffice. Most importantly, thank you for doing it all 'right now' even though you too apparently have a life of your own.

Thank you to my Mum and Dad (who probably will never see this – could someone give them a heads up please) for loving me, supporting me and championing everything I do even when they don't understand what it is I'm actually doing and why I don't just 'get a proper job'.

Judith Morgan - thank you for weaving your own very special brand of coaching magic, coming up with genius solutions and helping me to find the strength to follow my passion, pursue my dream and drink lots of green juice along the way.

Deborah Taylor – thank you for gently but firmly taking me by the hand and guiding me through the crazy maze of publishing protocol. Without your editorial expertise, wise counsel and generosity of time and attention I just would not have got to this stage, and this book would not be as polished as it is.

Jo Morgan and Jo Lord – thank you so much for being my first two unofficial reviewers. Your kind comments, detailed feedback and plentiful praise have spurred me on.

Thank you to all my fabulous friends (you know who you are – if you're wondering, then yes, it's you!) for the pub-based pep talks and wine-fuelled words of encouragement.

A huge thank you to all the amazingly awesome, the terrifyingly terrible and the disgracefully despicable work colleagues, managers and companies I've encountered during the last twenty years. Without you I would not have had the experiences that are included in this book or the impulse to share those experiences.

The biggest thank you is to YOU. Thank you for putting your faith in me and buying the book. Thank you for taking the time to read it. I hope it gives you some useful tips, a few smiles and shows you that you're not alone at the Horroffice, even when it feels as though you are.

Contents

Preparation for the Horroffice Meeting

Hello, and thanks for joining me. I've invited you to the Coping with the Horroffice meeting because I think we have a common problem, and I think we can work through it together.

I've worked in a lot of offices during my career and if you're reading this, the chances are you've done the same. Every day, five days a week, nine to five (if we're lucky) – it's where we spend the bulk of our time. It's also where we earn our pennies, forge friendships, experience career highs and lows, and emotional highs – some of us even fall in love at the office – and lows (some of us fall into the stationery cupboard for a drunken Christmas fumble!).

I've worked in awesome offices – fun, supportive, full of buzz – with beautiful people and brilliant brainstorming. But I've also worked in some truly awful, soul-sucking places. And I'm sure you have too.

And it was those horrendous places that got me thinking – when we join a new office we're taught how to use the coffee machine, we're shown where the toilets are and how to work the photocopier. We're taught what our job entails. What we're never taught is how to actually deal with office life. We're not shown how to manage crazy workloads. We're not taught how to deal with difficult colleagues. We're not taught how to deal with crappy days. Hands up if you recognise any of those!

And if you're unlucky enough to work in an office where you have to deal with more than one of these office issues, then it can feel like you're actually working in...the Horroffice.

And that's where this book comes in, because I've been there too and I have devised some solutions to those hair-tearing problems.

I started out as a lowly office junior. I've been part of large and small teams. I've spent a lot of time as a manager, so I've had to deal with pen-pushers, pedants and petty jobsworths, I know all about long hours and awkward money stuff. I've sometimes struggled to cope with the daily grind. In this book, I share with you some funny stories, some horror stories and plenty of different tricks, techniques and life lessons that I've picked up as I've battled a few of my Horroffices – and I guarantee you'll find them useful in whatever Horroffice situation you find yourself in.

So pull up a chair and join me in the first meeting of the Coping with the Horroffice Club.

Agenda – Coping with the Horroffice

Date:	Every day
Time:	9am–5pm (you hope)
Objective:	Finding ways to help you to cope with the Horroffice without going nuts
Meeting organiser:	Heena Pattni
Attendees:	You, me and some other office characters

Agenda Items

Item 1	Coping with Other People's Bullshit
Item 2	Coping with Other People's Happy
Item 3	Coping with Comparisons
Item 4	Coping with Money Stuff
Item 5	Coping with Self-Doubt
Item 6	Coping with Overwhelm
Item 7	Coping Mindfully
Item 8	Coping with Crappy Days
Item 9	Coping with Change
Item 10	Beyond Coping
Item 11	Any Other Business

Meeting Organiser

I know, I know. I can almost hear you groaning into your second (or is it third) cup of coffee. One of your colleagues has just thrust a copy of this book in front of your face, telling you, 'It's changed my life, like, COMPLETELY – she totally gets it!' And you're thinking, 'Yeah, yeah – same old, same old. Another "self-help" book that helps no-one (except the author)!' I'm right, aren't I?

Why did I write it? Honestly? Because I was where you are (and sometimes still find myself there) and, yes, it did help me – I hope it helps you too.

So how about I start by telling you a bit about me, the meeting organiser and author, and why I think I'm qualified to rescue you from your personal Horroffice.

I have a background in number crunching – I trained as an accountant. I graduated in a recession when jobs were hard to come by so I temped for a while, then I worked in small start-ups, one of which turned into a big player (after I left, of course), and eventually I went to work for a 'Big Four' accounting firm as an auditor for over thirteen years. I'm currently a finance contractor, so I move to a different company every six to twelve months. If you add all that up, it means I've worked in a lot of offices. I've seen some great places and some truly awful places, big companies and small ones. No one has ever quite seen it all, but I've seen a fair bit.

I've also been through a significant, serious illness not once but twice, and I'm now just over five years in remission from cancer. Getting through that has also given me some awesome insights and coping strategies.

Then there's my family and friends (real ones, not just the Facebook ones). Some of them work in offices and we talk, share our office experiences and commiserate – usually over copious glasses of red wine.

I've been on some fantastic training courses, some terrible courses and some mind-bogglingly boring ones (haven't we all?), gaining some excellent skills in mentoring, coaching, communication, relating to people, hypnotherapy and neuro-linguistic programming to name a few.

I've tried and tested lots of different techniques in my own search for a happier way to live: counselling, hypnotherapy, Emotional Freedom Technique, drinking into oblivion, boring friends and family with my problems, medication, meditation...you get the idea.

Now I've distilled all those experiences to share with you into this shoot-from-the-hip guide. I don't use airy-fairy language (I don't like it, and I sound like an idiot when I try to sound cleverer than I am). Instead I just outline the issue then explain my technique for coping with it so you understand why and how it could work just as well for you.

Just one word of warning before we start. You need to know that there's no single right answer, no wonder drug, no unique winning technique to coping with crap, especially office crap, because every situation is different. You need to make the judgement as to whether an individual technique will work for you. Some things will work better for some people, just because of the different ways we're all wired. It's about finding the right mix of stuff for you. That took me a long time to work out, and I want to save you some time. So go through the book at your own pace, pick out the bits you like the sound of, then give them a go.

But only give it a go if you can do so with an open mind. If you do that, it might work for you, it might not, but it'll be an honest assessment. If you go into it thinking, 'This is nonsense – it won't work', well then ... it won't work. Not because it's not a good technique, but because you've already decided it will fail. Your brain will find a way to make that true for you.

Meeting Attendees

So now you've met me, let's see who else is coming to our Coping with the Horroffice meeting.

Sam – the inept office junior

Eager, enthusiastic, slightly terrified and with no idea what he's doing, think of Sam as a six-month-old puppy. He only wants to make you happy, but the harder he tries to do that, the more chaos he causes.

The best way to deal with Sam is to take a deep breath and explain things carefully and in detail. Check in on him regularly to make sure he understands what you want. Lots of praise will help. Don't hit him on the nose if he does something naughty. (Apparently, according to HR, that's not allowed.) He needs to learn, and you'll reap the benefits if you take the time teach him your way.

Vera – the office long-termer

Vera has been at that desk since the beginning of time. She's seen it all, done it all and moans about it all. Although, despite the moaning, she's never looked for a job elsewhere.

The best way to deal with Vera is to let her tell you her history at least once, so she's got it out of her system. After that, try and keep conversations short and based on the here and now. If she starts to veer towards 'way back when' territory, head her off quickly and cleanly. Anything from, 'Oh yes, I loved your story about how you used papyrus scrolls but that's more than I could cope with – I only know how to scan! Could you get these done by lunch time?' to 'Sorry, Vera, but I absolutely must dash – need the loo.' She'll soon realise that you don't want to join her 'wallow with me' club.

Neil – the know-it-all

Neil's way isn't just the best way, it's the only way. He doesn't tolerate changes to his plan. (I can hear you sigh – we all know a Neil, don't we?)

The best way to deal with Neil will depend on whether he's your manager or your colleague. If he's your manager, then it's a case of persuading him that your way was his way all along. You also sell him on the benefits at the same time. You could say something like, 'Thanks for showing me how to do that. Do you also want me to do this, so it's done faster?' He'll love thinking he's improved on his own idea!

If Neil is a colleague, you could try the same technique – it's annoying but if you get your way in the end, who's won? But if that doesn't work, you could always go straight to your manager with your suggestion for improvement. Once he's given you the go ahead, it won't matter whether Neil wants to do it his way, you'll both be doing what your boss tells you to do.

Edna – the ideas thief

Often, without you quite realising what she's doing, Edna will find out your opinions in general conversation, then leap in at the team meeting and regurgitate all your ideas before you get a chance to open your mouth.

The best way to deal with Edna is simply not to engage with her. Don't be caught out twice. Tell her nothing. If she pushes, then tell her you're not sure, you haven't had a chance to consider it yet, or you are still formulating your ideas so you'll be ready for the meeting. Better still, turn the tables and ask her what ideas she's come up with. That's bound to send her scurrying away.

Tracey – the tattle-tale rumour-monger

You'll find Tracey at someone else's desk more often than her own, having a cosy, whispered chat, getting and giving the low-down on everyone else.

The best way to deal with Tracey is to stay polite and friendly but slightly aloof. It'll mean she gossips about you but, let's face it, that was going to happen anyway. On no account should you engage or ask her any questions; that'll just encourage more gossiping. Firm, friendly but distant is what you're aiming for.

Patsy – the passive-aggressive martyr

Always there before everyone else in the morning, always leaving after everyone in the evening, Patsy has a manic workload no matter how many hours she's putting in.

This is a bit of a toughie, and I talk about it in a bit more detail in Item 1.

The problem is that passive aggression is indirect, it's hidden. So the best way of dealing with it is to get it out in the open. Make sure you deal only with specifics, though. Generalising in a discussion with a passive-aggressive type leads to more problems. Pay attention to what Patsy does and what her results are, rather than what she says. If there's an issue with either of these, then you can discuss that issue. Patsy may have stayed late getting a report done, but if that means she left the payroll and now your creditors are yelling, there's a problem. She needs to get to grips with best practice in dealing with deadlines and communicating with colleagues. She needs to tell you beforehand one of the two goals is going to be missed, and ask for help. Telling you after the fact that she stayed five hours and works harder than everyone else is not helpful.

If you're Patsy's colleague, the same rules apply. If she says she always has to stay late and her workload is too much, suggest she needs to talk to the manager. Ask her exactly what she has on and how many hours she thinks it will take. Ask her for specific ways the team can help her balance her workload. But also ensure you point out the workload others in the team have, so she is aware she isn't the only one with an overflowing in-tray.

Dick – the overbearing, fire-breathing dragon boss

Dick wants results – and he'll shout until he gets them. He sees his team as annoying minions there to do his bidding, rather than human beings.

This is a tough one, because he's your boss. And also because you need to be strong to stand up for yourself. It's all possible, though. Remember that you aren't a minion, you're a human. You were employed because you can do the job and you deserve to be treated with respect.

If Dick dumps a whole load of work with unrealistic deadlines on your desk, check out Item 6. Work out a plan of what you can do when and take it to Dick. He needs to decide what he needs most – that's not your job.

If that doesn't stop him shouting, you'll need to tackle the issue head on. If you don't feel you can tell Dick you don't want to be shouted at, then email him. Compose your email when you are calm, not just after being yelled at, and draft it without filling in the recipient line (so you can't send it by mistake when it's not finished). Then leave it overnight and read it through before you send it. Keep the tone calm, the information to-the-point; highlight your professional competence and tell him you perform at your best when you are in a positive environment. If you are arranging a meeting, you could do this anyway to get your thoughts in order. Don't feel you can do that? Speak to HR – they'll tell him.

Item 1 – Coping with Other People's Bullshit

'Most people are other people. Their thoughts are someone else's opinions, their lives a mimicry, their passions a quotation.'

Oscar Wilde (1854–1900), Irish writer and poet

So one of the first, and definitely most important, things we need to deal with at the Horroffice is...other people.

We've all met them (and quite possibly been them). You've certainly seen some of them attending the Horroffice meeting. So you have this crazy mix of people, all with their different views on the office, the company and life in general. And every one of these people has their own agenda. Which is fine.

What you need to be wary of is getting sucked into those agendas.

Passive-aggressive bullshit

For example, it had been a while since I'd seen such a strong version of the passive-aggressive martyr, but in a recent contracting role, I came into contact with Patsy in a big way. Unfortunately she also happened to be the office b***h. I was very new to the company, and my predecessor had left without a handover – he hadn't even left any handover notes. I literally had no idea what to do and was learning bit by bit, day by day, at the same time as managing a team that was looking to me to lead them and look after them.

Patsy came across initially as hard-working, organised and just a bit cool. But after a couple of months, I noticed a pattern in how she dealt with things. She never offered any help or support. She would wait until something had gone wrong, something that she knew was going to go wrong. She would make sure no blame could be laid at her desk. Then, instead of coming to me with the issues – as she should, given that they related to my team – she'd email my boss and copy me in. Obviously, this made me and the team look incompetent, when actually I was just new and clueless. It also made her look knowledgeable and sharp.

After this had happened a couple of times, I got frustrated and annoyed, but I decided to play her at her own game. I went to my boss armed with the evidence from previous issues. I pointed out that if she had raised the alarm earlier in the game, I could have taken action and nothing would have gone wrong. It would have been a win-win situation rather than a lose-lose one, wasting time and effort.

I could do this because, luckily for me, my boss valued honesty. If he hadn't, it would have been a much tougher situation. As soon as I raised it, he admitted to me he was well aware of how she liked to cause trouble. She had a habit of running to him with every little thing anyone had done wrong. He knew she wasn't perfect, but he could overlook that because, in his eyes, she was such a hard worker – the long hours and martyred conversations had done their job. However, having the conversation with him meant we found a way to work where I was effectively able to cut her out of the loop and work directly with her manager, a much more reasonable guy. I'd taken the sting out of her tail.

You see what I mean. She had no reason to behave like that, except to make herself look good whilst making everyone else look bad. Her bullshit. Not mine, nor my team's. But it impacted us all the same. And it was exhausting, infuriating and demoralising having to deal with it every day.

Watch out for low blows

Another example I had of dealing with other people's agendas was at one of my earlier contracts. It was a lovely environment, a well-resourced finance function, and my manager ran it very well. His department was split in two in terms of work: I managed the accounting team, and there was another manager looking after the transactions team. She'd been at the company for a very long time and had clearly worked hard to move her way up. But I got the feeling she was stuck where she was because she didn't have any accounting qualifications and so couldn't take the next step. She ran a tight ship in her team, and the work was done on schedule.

We didn't have a huge amount of crossover, but we did have regular team meetings to make sure we were all aware of what everyone else was doing. I was always very impressed at how much work she had to deal with – she had put herself forward for a number of different projects, she was on the social committee and every meeting we had she was always the last one to turn up because she was so busy. She was also somewhat disparaging to our boss. She had two team leaders reporting in to her and they sometimes seemed to form a bit of a gang, often making snide comments and sniggering together. They always knew what was going on in other departments and gossiped incessantly. It was a bit like being back at school.

After a few weeks she invited me to the pub for lunch with her and the 'gang'. They asked about my background, shared some of theirs and then spent the rest of the hour telling me how useless our boss was, and how little they thought of him. I just said I hadn't worked with him long enough to see what they were talking about, and they laughed that it wouldn't be long before I did. Privately, I actually thought he was a great boss so far– thoughtful, intelligent and fair – but I didn't want to be thrown out of the 'gang' just as I'd been admitted.

A couple of days after that, just before our next big meeting, she sidled up to me for what seemed to be a little joke and chat, then she said how she was so busy she didn't have time for this meeting – what about me? I agreed I was busy too. She pounced. Why didn't I go up to our manager and tell him to postpone – I was busy, she was busy, I was new, he'd understand. But I'd already prepared and freed up the time, so I said I'd be okay working around it, although she was free to ask him herself if she really needed to move it. I got a little sigh and smile and the meeting went ahead. She tried the same tactic over a new policy he was implementing, but again the policy made sense to me, and I told her that. My lunch invitations stopped around then. I knew her well enough to understand that by not taking part in her agenda, I had now made myself a target, so I wasn't surprised when one of my team told me that when I'd been off for a day, she'd exclaimed about it loudly just as our boss was in earshot. Unluckily for her, I'd already told him I'd be away and why, so he was fine. I made sure I kept out of her way as much as possible, and always brought extra-thick skin to work in case of low-blow rumours, and she eventually got bored and moved on to another target.

Make it all about the work

So next time someone seems to be going out of their way to make things tough for you, remember that they're generally doing it because of their own baggage, their own issues, their own neuroses.

It's not your bullshit so don't let yourself get covered in it.

What is important is that you take emotion and other people's agendas out of it – make it only about the work. That will start to defuse the situation, because emotion or gossip is what Patsy Passive-Aggressive and Tracey Tattle-Tale thrive on. If your boss won't help, then go to your HR department. Handle it as early as you can, so you can nip it in the bud before it gets overgrown.

I know we can't avoid it all the time, but the actions below will help you cope a bit better. (I find a large glass or two of rosé helps me release the tension on a more immediate basis, too!)

Actions – Goals

It's easy to get distracted by other people's bullshit if you don't have your own agenda.

Set goals, control your future

A good way to avoid getting sucked into other people's bullshit is to have a clear picture of why you are where you are, doing what you're doing, and what that's going to lead to. It's a bit like this.

Imagine your life is a car. Setting goals and following through on them is like you taking the steering wheel, setting the GPS and deciding on your destination. It stops other people hijacking your car to get them to their destination instead (you might offer them a lift if it's on the way, but that's your call, not theirs).

Set goals, create purpose

When you know what your own life purpose is, you feel stronger, more confident, and you can make better choices because those choices are guided by that purpose. Setting goals helps you clarify that purpose because they are there to help you on the way. When you set yourself clear goals, you're not just driving your car aimlessly. You know where you're going and that helps you navigate your way with purpose.

Set goals, increase your motivation

When you set goals, you also give yourself a little challenge, a little dare, a little buzz. You're in competition with the only person worth competing against – yourself. Creating goals for yourself gives you something to aim for, to push towards and that's sometimes the impetus we need to get off our backsides and get on with it.

Tips – Defining Your Goals

Goals have to be quite specific if they are to succeed in motivating you. Avoid things like, 'I want to do well' – you can do better than that!

Tip 1 – Make them your own goals

The goals you set for yourself aren't necessarily the 'objectives' listed at your annual appraisal – these are the company's or your manager's goals for you. These goals are your own personal reasons for being in this job, in this company, at this time. Be clear on why you think you are in the job and where you think it will take you. Ask yourself a series of questions and be honest in your answers. Why did you decide to join the company? What is it you'll gain in terms of experience, knowledge, training? How will you know you're achieving those goals? What does success look like and feel like for you?

Tip 2 – Make them SMART

You've probably seen the acronym a million times but that's because it's a good one. You want to make your goals:

S   Specific – if they are vague, they are dreams. "I want to do well" versus "I want to make manager level."

M   Measurable – then you know when you have achieved them. Again, if your goal is 'doing well' how do you know you're there? 'Making manager' is much easier to measure – you know when it's happened.

A   Attainable – what's the point of setting yourself a goal that's impossible to achieve? (I want to be a billionaire CEO is attainable with the right effort and time. I want to be a green leprechaun with fairy wings is, sadly, not.)

R   Realistic – high goals can be great but you still have to make them realistic. If you are targeting that CEO job, work backwards and break it down into manageable chunks so you have a series of goals that will make this happen.

T   Time bound – give yourself a timeframe to work in, with a slight sense of urgency so you don't lose motivation. "I want to make manager in the next twelve months" gives you a greater sense of focus than "I want to make manager soon."

Tip 3 – Take it step by step

A goal, especially a challenging one, can seem overwhelming – as if there's a huge gap between where you are and where you want to be.

But it will start to appear less daunting if you break it down into manageable steps. Look at how you'll work towards it and establish a realistic timeline.

When you look at everything you have to do to get there, it can feel like it's a gargantuan task. A way to combat that is to forget everything except the next step. Take action towards your goal every day, even if you only do something small or spend a short time on it – half an hour a day is better than nothing.

Each action is a step, each step takes you further along the path, until eventually you'll turn around and see how much you've achieved because you worked on one step at a time without being distracted by the bigger picture.

Item 2 – Coping with Other People's Happy

'*To be happy, we must not be too concerned with others.*'

Albert Camus (1913–1960), French Nobel Prize winning
author, journalist and philosopher

It's a similar idea to Item 1 but we're coming at it from the other side of the fence. My experiences taught me to cope with Other People's Happy, which isn't always the same as your Happy.

You'll have heard it plenty of times over the years; it's the list of things that should make you happy. And apparently it's only those things should make you happy. If you accidentally get happy from stuff not on the list, it doesn't count. In which case, you must immediately stop being happy and find out how to get the permitted happy stuff that's on the list.

What did you say? The stuff on the list doesn't work for you? Ah, what a shame. You'd better resign yourself to being miserable for the rest of your life (and monitor the Other People's Happy list in case any of your 'weird' happy sneaks onto the list).

My happy is not your happy

The first time I remember it happening at work was in my very first permanent role. I'd started as an accounts assistant. It was a great first job – I learned loads and really got stuck into the role. But about eighteen months later, I got itchy feet. I'd achieved everything I could in the job and I wanted to develop. My boss had other ideas, however. She wanted me to stay where I was because I was a good worker, I got things done and she didn't have to worry about my area.

So when I applied for a role internally within the organisation, she was very discouraging. And the day I went for the interview, her boss, our finance director, came over and told me that no matter what happened I would always have my role as an assistant – they could even move me to be an assistant in a slightly different area. Without actually spelling it out, they were saying the only way to go was sideways.

I didn't get the other internal role. But I knew I didn't want to stay in the same job for ever, and I also knew that I wouldn't be allowed to move upwards … so I moved out. Ultimately, they lost a hard worker, and they lost the knowledge, training and development time they'd already invested in me, which seemed a bit short-sighted.

I remember my manager's words at my exit interview: 'You're just jumping out of the frying pan into the fire, Heena. You won't enjoy it.' Hmmm. I think that might have been sour grapes because I'd chosen to go with my own happy rather than theirs.

Later on in my career, towards the end of my time as an audit manager, I remember thinking that actually I was pretty happy in the particular role I was in. I'd developed some specialist knowledge, I liked most of my clients, I had a decent variety of work and a good work-life balance. But just as I thought, 'Yes – I can stay here for a while', the powers that be had other ideas. They wanted me to focus on areas I wasn't interested in. In the Big 4 firms (at that time anyway), it was about moving onwards and upwards – or out. Even if you were good at what you did and happy there, you had to keep moving. But I didn't want to move onwards in the direction I was being pushed. And I definitely didn't want to move upwards. I'd seen how much more stressful it was one level up and I didn't want that.

Again, my idea of happy was not the same as theirs. And it was a real blessing that I was pushed, because again, instead of pushing me upwards, it pushed me to think about what I really wanted. And what I really wanted was out.

Looking back, I'm actually grateful to both sets of employers because if they hadn't behaved the way they did, I might not be doing what I'm doing now – writing, enjoying the freedom of contracting, living my life on my terms.

Follow your own path

So what I'd say is this – you need to be careful that you're not just following the path other people want you to follow, a path that suits their agenda, unless it's also a path that suits your agenda.

Make sure that before you make a decision, you check in with the goals you've set for yourself. Will your decision help you towards those goals or will it steer you further away?

It's not always easy when you choose to go against the flow of Other People's Happy. You'll get dire warnings of things falling apart for you, as well as heavy sighs and frowns. But that's just because your choice is causing a problem for someone else. That's not your problem. Or as a lovely quote I read recently stated: 'Not my monkeys. Not my circus.'

Look after your own monkeys and your own circus, no matter what anyone else says. The rest is up to them. And when you stop worrying about other people's responsibilities, you'll find the world still goes on turning. The sky is still above your head and the ground below. Nothing has fallen apart. It's all cool.

Actions – Stop 'Should'ing

Watch out for a simple code word that is often slipped into conversations when other people see you veering away from what they want you to do. The code word is 'should'. We don't always notice we're doing it, but whenever you find yourself 'should'ing, try these tips to stop.

'Should have' less, stress less

Every time you say 'I should have...' to yourself (whether it's aloud in conversations or just in your own thoughts) what you're actually telling yourself is that you've failed. You're saying that you held yourself up to a standard and didn't meet it. This is not helpful. In fact, it will just make you feel even more stressed. 'I should have spoken up in that meeting', 'I should have offered to stay and do some overtime', 'I should have got to the office earlier'.

It's possible that achieving these things would have helped you at work, but it's not the end of the world. And by going over what you 'should' have done, you are focusing on a mental picture of failure. That picture isn't helpful, so banish the 'should'.

'Should' less, 'want' more

We've become so used to listening to the 'should' police, we've forgotten how to think for ourselves. We think we 'should' want that promotion, or that new job, or we 'should' take on more work, we 'should' agree with the suggestion our boss made, even if we don't think it's a good idea, we 'should' stay in a job we hate because we trained for years in that field. But what if you took a 'should' holiday, just for an afternoon or a day – what would you actually *want* to do then? Even if it wasn't on the 'should' list, what would make it on to your 'want' list?

'Should' less, take back control

It's true in life we can't always avoid the 'should' – as in I 'should' eat spinach and kale when what I really want is to eat chocolate. But we need to test that 'should' to make sure we are in control. Look the decision square in the face and understand why that particular 'should' is important to us.

This one is important because there's a bigger, more alluring want – I *want* to feel good in my body, I *want* to be healthy and enjoy life. I 'should' stay in this job that I hate because I *want* to provide for my family, and right now this is the best way to do that. Just knowing why we're accepting those particular 'shoulds' gives us back control, focus and maybe even some motivation.

Tips – Banish the "Should"

Start to retrain yourself not to use this simple little word – it is more powerfully negative than it looks.

Tip 1 – Take a 'should' break

It doesn't have to be a long one, but if you can find a little bit of time, ideally every day, to take a break from what you 'should' do or be, and just go and do or be what you 'want', it helps bring a little joy back into your life.

Tip 2 – Unravel the 'should'

When you find yourself 'should'ing, stop and break it down. Ask yourself *why* you should be doing what you think you should be doing? What is the point of the 'should'? What will that 'should' lead you to? Once you have that, look at the answer and assess whether it's really something that ties in with your goals, or whether it's just someone else's idea that's snuck into your head and onto your to-do list.

Tip 3 – Don't be a 'should', be an 'I am'

'Should' is negative – it lacks energy, motivation, excitement. 'I should work on that proposal for another hour' doesn't sound exhilarating does it? If you really 'should' do something, then change the way you think – and talk - about it. It will change the way you feel about it, too. So change 'I should work on that proposal for another hour' to 'I am going to get this proposal done in the next hour' – it has more focus, energy and determination. If you really *have* to do something, rephrase it from an 'I should...' to an 'I am going to...' and that will lead to better results.

Item 3 – Coping with Comparisons

'When you are content to be simply yourself and don't compare or compete, everybody will respect you.'

Lao Tzu (604–531BC), Chinese philosopher, poet, author
and founder of Taoism

It starts when we're very young. At school, we're measured, compared, put into sets, measured again, graded, judged. And it carries on through college, university and throughout our working lives. Am I better/faster/more efficient than my colleagues? What appraisal grade did they get? Why is it higher than mine? How much overtime are they doing? How much am I doing? What does my boss think of that? You get the idea.

Confounding expectations

I had an appraisal meeting three months after I'd recovered from cancer for the second time. I don't remember many of my appraisal meetings over the years, but this one I don't think I'll ever forget.

My appraiser pulled out a piece of paper containing a list of all the managers in my department and how many standard hours, overtime hours and sickness hours they'd logged. He pointed out to me that I was at the wrong end of the scale for both the sickness and overtime hours, and that there were managers who were putting in more overtime than I was putting in standard hours.

The implication was obvious but also shocking. I had just come back from a serious, significant illness so of course my sickness was going to be high. And after recovering, did he really expect me to work myself back into another illness just so that I could be 'average'? Apparently so. Except this time, I wasn't having any of it. I believe my response was, 'Well somebody's got to be at the wrong end of the range, haven't they?' He didn't know what to say to that. I hadn't been embarrassed into promising to work longer hours.

But there it was again – we were being measured, compared, judged and, in this case, found wanting. I had been graded down. Apparently my illness had been taken into account, although no figures were forthcoming to justify that statement. It was a nail in the coffin of my auditing career.

There are two sides to this, of course. I completely understand that the work needs to be completed quickly and efficiently, and it is only fair that everyone pulls their weight.

When I was booking staff to complete audits for me, I would, of course, choose the most efficient from those available because I needed to get the work done. However, I don't think that has to be inconsistent with treating your employees as human beings rather than humans doing. In the end I believe it leads to a happier team and better productivity.

And that's what *you* need to remember. Ultimately your employer, whether benevolent or a ball-breaker, is just looking to get the job done. If they're conscientious, they'll also be looking to broaden your skills and experience. But only if it fits in with their ultimate goals. And in getting the job done, they will inevitably compare you to others.

The only valid comparison

That doesn't mean *you* have to compare yourself to others. Your situation and circumstances are different from everyone around you. It's not realistic to put two people in the same environment with the same tools and necessarily expect exactly the same outcome. Even twins would perform differently from each other because we all come with our own motivation, baggage, skills, issues.

So when an employer is measuring you, comparing you, judging you, remember that they're not actually comparing YOU. Not you as a person. They're just comparing your end product to your colleagues' end products. You don't need to buy into the comparison.

The only person you can ever really compare yourself to is you. Are you doing better than you were this time last year? How have you developed? What have you learned? What do you still need to focus on and fine tune?

When I left my audit manager role (and probably a while before, around the time of that infamous appraisal), I stopped comparing myself to everyone else and just compared myself to me. It was a game changer for me.

The decisions I make now are based on whether an action or a choice will make me happier, get me closer to my own goals or take me the other way. I don't care what other people are doing; I only care how I'm doing, whether I'm in a better place than I was in the past and whether I'm moving closer to my goals.

And that's all you need to focus on. As long as you're improving when you compare yourself today to how you were yesterday, that's okay. That's progress.

Actions – The Wheel of Life

You may have come across the Wheel of Life (WoL) already, but it doesn't hurt to repeat something good, does it?

Use the WoL to stop comparing

The first thing using the Wheel of Life (WoL) does is to stop you comparing yourself to other people. It brings all your focus back on you. The WoL doesn't care how your manager feels about things; it doesn't care what the impact of all that overtime is doing to your colleague's family life. The WoL is all about you and only you.

Use the WoL to achieve focus

Once you start using the WoL, it gives you clarity and focus. You know exactly where you are in each of the areas of life that are important to you. It gives you a very visual representation of how happy you're feeling in each aspect of your life, and how that's working for you overall.

And remember, the idea isn't to beat yourself up if you find an area is showing up lower that you'd like. That sounds painful, unnecessary and unhelpful.

The idea is that you know exactly where you can focus your considerable efforts next.

Use the WoL and take action

Once you've completed the wheel, use that knowledge to work out what to focus on, what you want to change to help you feel happier. And then decide on the actions that will help to get you there.

Tips – Balancing the Wheel

You can use the same principles to draw up any kind of chart or diagram that highlights the strengths and the areas that need a bit more attention in your life.

Tip 1 – Drawing up your wheel

Create a pie chart divided into the segments that are crucial to your life. Don't just use the ones I've chosen if they don't match what's important to you.

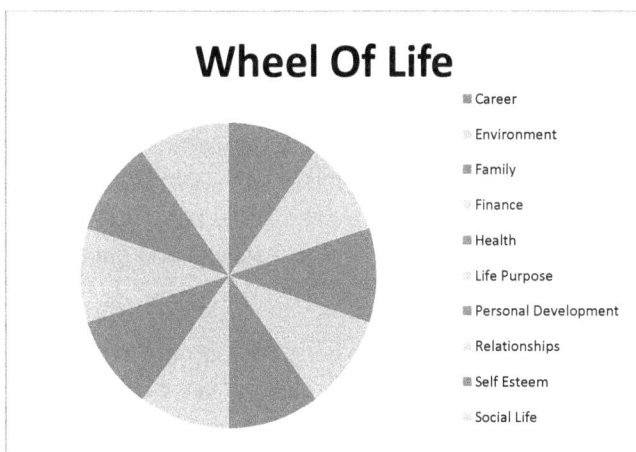

Wheel Of Life

■ Career
▨ Environment
■ Family
▨ Finance
■ Health
▨ Life Purpose
■ Personal Development
▨ Relationships
■ Self Esteem
▨ Social Life

Then use a score of zero to ten – zero being in the middle and ten on the circumference – to score how you feel you are doing in that aspect of your life. Plot all your scores on the chart.

Tip 2 – Reflecting on your chart

Remember, the chart is just a tool to help you focus and work out where you are, where you want to be, and what's important to you. It helps you to see where your life might be out of balance. Ideally you want all the scores to be relatively high, so you have a lovely wheel that's rotating nicely, moving your life forward in a smooth way.

Tip 3 – Take action

If you find that your wheel is lopsided, then it gives you a chance to do something about it.

For example, if you scored yourself seven on everything except Social life and Personal development, and you'd scored these at three and five, then your wheel is going to be a bit lopsided. Focus on those areas and think about what you could do to even things up – maybe call a few friends you haven't seen in a while and arrange a few nights out. Or invest in a course that interests you and encourages some personal development and growth.

And when you're doing this, don't be too hard on yourself. This isn't an exam. You don't pass or fail. It's just a very visual way of helping you see what's working and making you happy and what you might want to focus on a bit more.

And every few weeks or months (whatever works for you) but at least once a year, take stock. Re-assess your Wheel of Life and see how far you've come.

Item 4 – Coping with Money Stuff

'Money is only a tool. It will take you wherever you wish, but it will not replace you as the driver.'

Ayn Rand (1905–1982), Russian-American novelist, philosopher, playwright and screenwriter

Money is another tool we use to compare ourselves. We are reticent to talk about it openly to anyone else (especially if, like me, you're British) but we care about it an awful lot.

It goes a bit like this: 'How much am I earning? How much is Fred earning? Because Fred does what I do, but I do it better. But he's been here longer. But that shouldn't count, should it? So what does Fred earn, then? I need to know so I know whether I can be happy with what I earn.' Does any of that sound familiar?

Money is a means, not an end

I remember an audit partner saying something to me when I was moaning to him about the poor bonus I had been given that year (and yes, it was less than some of my peers, but more than others). He told me that he always expected the least, so that anything he got was a bonus.

Now the cynic in me knows that's a useful ploy to keep the troops quiet. It's the old 'promise nothing and deliver a bit –

it'll seem like you've delivered loads' con. But actually, there is a grain of usefulness in it too.

Money is necessary. There's no getting around that. But money shouldn't be the yardstick by which we measure ourselves. If you measured the worth of Mahatma Gandhi just on his net assets when he died, he wouldn't have come out so well. But measuring his contribution to India, to the world? A completely different story. And whilst I'm not advocating we eschew money completely, it shouldn't be the only tool you use when measuring yourself at the office – or in life, in general either.

A few years into my auditing career, when I was an audit senior, the company was trying to manage in a difficult economy and decided to offer sabbaticals. I jumped at the chance. It was the perfect opportunity to take three months to write my bestseller (unfortunately procrastination came on the sabbatical too, but that's another tale for another day). A lot of people, in and out of the office, advised me not to do it. They were all worried it would be seen as a negative thing, as proof that I wasn't committed to the firm. Plus no-one was too keen on the 'no money for three months' thing.

In one way, they were right. It was seen that way by the company, and I did have to economise for a few months. But that was okay; I was happy to trade in some money in the bank for three months of living as a writer, three months of joy. And I started to realise that my self-value wasn't just connected to my bank balance.

The year before I was promoted to audit manager, I was headhunted by another of the Big 4. Out of curiosity I went through the process and, surprising myself, I was offered a role heading up a new department. They were offering more money, a car, a better title, and the base office was marginally closer than my current one – a lot of advantages I didn't have at the time. Not only that, but I was a little disgruntled with my existing situation. The rose-tinted specs had come off a while ago and I wasn't feeling particularly appreciated. I handed in my notice.

Pros and cons are not just financial

But then my employers started trying to talk me round and it got me thinking, which got me in a muddle. When I still couldn't decide, I reached for my trusty tool – a list! I wrote down the pros and cons of the new job against the pros and cons of the old job. The title and salary I've already mentioned, but apart from that, the pros of the new job didn't quite measure up to what I already had. The disadvantages at the new place were higher too. So when I really stopped and thought about what I was giving up, I decided it wasn't worth the extra cash or flashy title. It opened my eyes to the fact the opportunities I had available where I was were actually pretty good, I just wasn't choosing to make the most of them.

I didn't want to measure myself solely by how much was coming into my bank account – development opportunities, variety of role, support, the valuable contacts and networks I'd built up all factored in to my decision. And to this day I stand by that decision – I was at the same company for 13 years, all through choice, and most of it happy. I think I did okay.

Remember, money is an essential companion, but the direction and drive should come from you.

Actions – Fix Your Finance Issues

Managing our finances affects every one of us, but we're never actually taught how to handle our money or our feelings around money. Most people are financially illiterate, and that makes for uncomfortable living.

Fix your finance issues, stress less

When we're constantly juggling our money, when we don't know whether we'll be able to cover this month's bills or next month's rent, when one broken appliance can set us back for weeks, it's not pleasant. Living with financial uncertainty isn't fun. It's stressful, painful and often unnecessary. Get financially savvy and save yourself sleepless nights worrying about your money.

Fix your finance issues, make better decisions

If you don't know what's going on in your bank account, if you wait for all the bills to be paid and spend what's left over, how can you make strong financial decisions? And if you can't make strong financial decisions, they'll impact on the way you live for the rest of your life. You have already established your goals. If you then know what you spend on essentials and what have left to play with each month, you can start to make financial decisions that will help you reach your goals.

Fix your finance issues, get more bang for your buck

If you know where your money is going, you can also decide whether that's working out for you, or whether you should be spending it/saving it/investing it somewhere else. And by fixing your finances you're also less likely to incur financial penalties, meaning you're holding on to more of your precious pennies. You've worked hard for your money, so make sure your money is working hard for you.

Tips – Managing Your Financial Mindset

It's not always the amount of money you have; it's what you do with it that is important.

Tip 1 – Get a goal

One thing I didn't have for a very long time was a long-term financial goal. I knew I wanted not to have to worry about money, and I knew I wanted some savings but that was about it. And not having financial goals is expensive, because in their absence, it's easy to forget about the future and just focus on having fun now.

But it definitely won't be fun when it's time to buy your first house and you don't have a deposit. Or when you need to find the cash for a new car and you've blown it all. Or even worse, when you get to retirement age and can't afford to stop working.

So establish your financial goals. Where do you want to be in ten years' time? How do your financial goals tie in with your other life goals? Once you know whether it's a car, a retirement plan or a holiday that's your priority, you can start thinking about how to get there.

Tip 2 – Stop comparing your in and their out

One of the reasons we get ourselves into a state about money is because we see what everyone else has – shiny new car, big house, new clothes – and we want that. We are likely to feel a bit miserable if we can't afford that. But you're not comparing like for like.

You're looking at their shiny pretty outsides and comparing it to your inside. You can't see that their credit card debts are the same as the GDP of a small nation. You can't see the panic and worry when another bill comes in.

Even if they can afford it, you have no idea how happy that's actually making them. You don't always see the long hours in the office or the arguments because they have a shiny car but the family next door have a shiny car and three holidays abroad. All you see is the surface. It's far better just to focus on your own goals and how your money situation is helping or hindering you.

Tip 3 – Don't use money as a measure of yourself

We all make the mistake of using money as a way of measuring ourselves, which is just plain wrong. That's not what money is for. I know that when I'm struggling financially I feel worse about myself. I feel worried about meeting the bills, annoyed I've let myself get into this state, and frustrated that I can't do all the things I want to right now.

But what I have to keep remembering is that my friends and family don't judge me based on my financial prowess. They don't say, 'Okay, Heena, we want to invite you out for drinks, but only if you have £XX in the bank.' (If you ever think a so-called friend thinks like that, ditch 'em fast!)

Money doesn't take into account any of the cool stuff that makes you so awesome. Using it as a measure of your value is like using a colander to measure water: messy and pointless. Don't do it.

Item 5 – Coping with Self-Doubt

'It is one of the most beautiful compensations of this life that no man can sincerely try to help another without helping himself.'

Ralph Waldo Emerson (1803–1882), essayist, author and poet

With all this being measured and judged and compared and monetised, it's no surprise that our self-belief takes a bit of a battering from time to time. One of my biggest fears at work was that I would be discovered to be a fraud. I was convinced I wasn't as good as people said I was, and definitely not as good as I was pretending to be, with my flashy lists and colour-coded tick sheets. That led me to sell myself short. I didn't push for promotions or pay rises. I stood back as colleagues got the cushier or more high-profile roles, convincing myself that was not what I wanted. And I believed it even more readily because it was partly true – I never wanted to be an accountant at all, so what right did I have to be a high-flying one?

But that's not a helpful attitude. As we've discussed already, employers need you to get the work done and the product or service delivered as efficiently as possible. Ideally, they'd like to pay you as little as possible whilst working you as long and hard as possible to achieve that so they can make oodles of cash. So they'll readily let you undervalue your own self-worth if it suits their purpose. There have only been a handful of people during my career who have both seen past my own self-sabotage and encouraged me to do something about it. Which is understandable because if I don't respect myself enough to believe in my own abilities, why should anyone else? That's changing now, but it hasn't been an easy ride.

Judge yourself fairly

I was part of a group of eight third year audit students who all passed our exams and were due to be promoted to the next level, assistant managers. I'd been given an average grading that year, and indications were that I would get the promotion. On the 1st October we all got our letters giving us details of our promotion and pay rise. I had been awarded a significant amount less than my peers, as had one of my colleagues. The reason? We had studied with a different accountancy body than the others. We'd done the same work, delivered on our clients and were graded as average, right in the middle of our peer group. But the firm was being cheeky and thought they could get away with a tenuous excuse like that. And if it had just been me, they would have. I was already very conscious of the fact that I was a 'Certified' accountant rather than a 'Chartered' accountant (although it actually made no real difference – we all did the same work). And I already felt a fraud. So although I felt cheated, I would have lived with it.

Believe in your own abilities

Luckily for me, the colleague who was in the same situation had none of these doubts. She was furious, and she dragged me in with her when she went to complain that it was unfair. She argued that we were doing the same job, doing it just as well as everyone else, and we deserved the same pay rise and promotion benefits. Her self-belief not only won us both a fair promotion but it also taught me a really valuable lesson. People will believe you're worth what you believe you're worth, whichever way you go with that.

I learnt more about the power of self-belief when I was contracting. When I took on my first contract, I still had the same mind-set – I didn't really believe in myself and my own abilities – but the six months of that contract changed my attitude. Because I didn't have to worry about office politics, or winning promotions or any of the things I was uncomfortable with in previous jobs, I could concentrate on just doing what I was paid to do. I did it well, and they thought I'd done a great job That meant I went into the next contract with a little less self-doubt which, in turn, meant I got even better results.

By the time I finished my last contract, even though I really didn't enjoy working for the company, I realised I really did have the ability to do a great job. See that – I said great, not just good or okay – I had made a positive impact and implemented changes that I hope will benefit the team for a long time to come.

Even if you doubt yourself, act as if you know what you're doing, as if you're the best person for the job. You WILL see results. Other people will believe you and more importantly, as you see results, you'll start to believe in yourself. And then you won't be acting, you'll just BE. There's one important caveat, of course: you have to deliver the goods. Don't try to impress if you genuinely have no clue.

Actions – Supercharge Your Confidence

Confidence in who you are and what you are doing is where it's at. Nail that and success will follow.

More self-confidence, cope with stress better

When the world around you becomes chaotic or stressful, as we all know it does (for me it was month-end at my various contracting roles that was the crazy time), having a healthy dose of self-confidence helps you to cope with that stress much better. Having the knowledge that you can cope with the situation actually allows you to cope with the situation well – it's self-perpetuating.

When you're not confident about how you'll cope, you worry more, you panic, you make decisions that aren't sound because they're based on fear and anxiety. And then the difficult situation you're in actually nosedives and becomes worse. This in turn just proves to you that you can't cope – that self-perpetuation kicks in just when you least need it.

When you have the self-confidence to think, 'I can handle this', your decisions come from a place of calm and strength and are more likely to have a positive impact, proving that you can cope.

More self-confidence, more positive contributions at work

When you have a healthy level of self-confidence, you tend to be more willing and able to take on challenging or difficult tasks, because you feel you can cope with (or even enjoy) them. You're also more likely to ask for help when you need it. You're confident in the knowledge that you can't know everything, and it's better to ask early than stay silent and get it wrong. Healthy self-confidence also allows you to spread your knowledge and positive attitude, something your peers, junior and managers will notice. No matter where you are in the workforce, the positive results emanating from being self-confident will get noticed!

More self-confidence, more ambition

Understandable, really. Having a strong sense of your own self-worth and your own abilities makes you more likely to aim high, because you'll be strong in the knowledge that what you're aiming for is achievable. And because you have a healthy dose of confidence, you'll find it easier to cope with the setbacks which undoubtedly come with aiming high. Instead of seeing such setbacks as a reason to give up, confident people use them as learning experiences. They learn, adapt and grow from difficult challenges and in doing so bolster their self-belief, moving them further towards their goals.

Tips – Believing in Yourself

There are many ways to boost you confidence and bolster your self-esteem. Here are a few to try out. I'm sure you'll come up with more ways that will work for you.

Tip 1 – Dress to impress

Hardly a new idea: dress to impress, dress for the job you want, not the job you're in. That doesn't matter. The reason you've heard it so often that it has become a cliché is because it works. When I first became an audit junior, I didn't really dress all that well. I wore suits because we had to, but they were cheap and did not fit all that well. I never really made much effort with my hair or the way I looked. I thought it was all about the work. And it *was* about the work, but that wasn't the whole picture.

My mum moaned at me for looking like a suited, booted bag lady (I know, mums, eh!). And I'd read something in *Cosmopolitan* magazine about dressing for the job you want. So I invested in some new clothes – a couple of sharper suits, and some nice heels – nothing over the top, but better than what I had been wearing.

I dressed a bit smarter and made a bit more of an effort (just an extra ten minutes in the morning). It worked. I felt a whole lot better about myself. I felt more empowered. I started behaving a little more confidently, because I felt smarter and sharper than before. And guess what? People started to take more notice at work. In fact, the first time I did it, someone asked me if I had an interview that day. Try it and see what you think.

Tip 2 – Kill the fear

I came across an acronym that I love: FEAR = False Expectations Appearing Real. I reckon at least ninety per cent of what we worry about just doesn't happen. So all that energy we've used worrying about it is wasted and we end up feeling depleted and our self-confidence takes a battering. Instead, try diverting that energy into just doing what you're worried about and getting it out of the way.

For example, I once worked at a company that was overwhelmingly negative. When my first team meeting was coming up, I knew there would be grumbles and moans. I worried that my team would think I was useless, that I couldn't cope, and I kept thinking of excuses for postponing the meeting.

But I was the manager and the meeting had to happen. So I prepared an agenda, took a deep breath and went for it. Yes, a lot of people moaned about things, but I made sure I kept the responses honest, realistic and, above all, positive. I gave them a chance to air their grievances, then I told them what we could change and what we had to find a way to deal with. Consequently, the meeting went much better than I thought it would.

From then on, I decided that's how I would approach each of my meetings at this company. People were going to moan regardless of what I did – that was the culture there – but I didn't have to be one of those people. I had to be me. If I could do something to make things better I would. If I'd made a mistake, I accepted it and changed, and if things had to stay as they were, I told the team. It made life a lot easier for me and a lot less exhausting.

Another positive that came from this new attitude was that so many of the things I thought would be raised at the meeting were never mentioned – they were all in my imagination so my worry really was a complete waste of time and energy.

The more I behaved as though I could handle anything, the more I found I *could* handle anything. FEAR: False Expectations Appearing Real. Get rid of. End of.

Tip 3 – Take a self-confidence inventory

One of the things that happens when you doubt yourself in one area is that you start to let it affect everything else that you do. Self-doubt is a nasty virus; it grows quickly and unexpectedly in all sorts of places. From 'I'm rubbish at this task', you can quickly find yourself at 'I'm just rubbish at everything!' So here's a way to nip it in the bud.

Get a piece of paper and draw a line down the middle. On the left-hand side, list ten strengths you feel you have and on the right-hand side list ten areas you want to improve on. If you're feeling down, ten strengths seem like a huge number, but you have more than that in the bag, trust me. If you're struggling for them, think about what other people have said, what they've complimented you on: 'Thanks for being a great friend, a good listener' – that is a strength. It doesn't matter how small the strength is, note it down anyway.

Now, rip the paper along that line. Keep the strengths somewhere you can see them every day – in your purse or wallet, on your bedside table, on the fridge.

That's your self-confidence inventory. It shows that although you might think you're rubbish at everything, you're actually very good at a lot of stuff. And it gives you some personal goals to work on. As you develop your skills, your confidence and yourself you'll soon be able to cross off some of the items on the weakness side and move them to your strength inventory.

Item 6 – Coping with Overwhelm

'It is your reaction to adversity, not the adversity itself, which determines how your life's story will develop.'

Dieter F. Uchtdorf (b. 1940), German aviator, airline executive and religious leader

No matter how cool your office, how awesome your colleagues and how supportive your boss, there will still be times when you feel completely overwhelmed with the amount of work you have to do.

Not enough hours in the day

As an audit manager who specialised in pension scheme audits, I ended up with a huge portfolio of clients. Of the fifty-odd clients I had at one point, thirty of them had their financial deadline on the same date. Luckily, I'm a natural organiser, so I found a way to cope. There was still a period of about two months though, when even with all the organising in the world I was still really struggling. Struggling to get things done, to keep the clients happy and to keep the work flowing.

My colleagues were in the same boat, as was my boss. So although we could empathise with each other, we couldn't necessarily lessen the burden for each other. And we couldn't fail a single one of our clients – it wasn't an option.

For those two months we burned ourselves out completely. We worked hard and we worked all hours. It was not fun.

At times it really was overwhelming. Even though we knew it was going to happen and were as prepared as we could be, things still went wrong: juniors went off sick or the client didn't have things ready for us. There were so many variables and we were all on such tight schedules and budgets that it wouldn't take very much for the whole lot to come tumbling down; that was overwhelming. At the time, we coped by moaning to each other, drinking copious amounts of coffee and working too many hours. But it's not healthy to do that in the long-term, and that level of stress is one of the reasons I left: overwhelm.

I also remember coaching a very junior team member who was struggling with a heavy case load of clients and didn't seem to be getting through the work. He had got into such a state of overwhelm that all he could see was a mountain of auditing and no way around or through it. Each time he picked up a file, he spent his time panicking about other work he should have been doing instead of getting on with what he needed to do. Many jobs were left half-finished. Clients were calling to hassle him, managers were demanding updates, promises were made and inevitably broken, leading to more hassle and recriminations. He was in a complete state of overwhelm.

In one of my recent contracts, a junior in my team had a very similar issue. When I joined the company, my first impression of him was that he was not particularly competent. His desk was always a complete mess, he regularly promised to deliver and then failed to meet agreed deadlines, and much of his time was spent complaining either to his colleagues or to me. He was making silly mistakes, which then took him forever to fix, stressing him still more so he was off sick on a regular basis. I needed to find a solution, so I took a closer look at what was going on.

Because he was so disorganised, he had no real idea of how to plan his day and consequently spent his whole time fire-fighting. Instead of being proactive and planning how to improve his workload, he dealt with whichever problem came with the loudest shout – which was not always the most important one. He made no secret of the fact he was looking elsewhere for work, although in the whole time I was there he was not successful in his search. He even applied for a role as a senior, thinking this would be a way to get rid of his workload, but this was at a time that he was performing so poorly that he had to be put on a development plan. Crazy, right? Again, the cause of all this was complete and total overwhelm.

Plan your way out of overwhelm

There may be a temptation to say that you don't have time to stop and reassess the situation, but that's exactly what you have to do. In the case of both the juniors, I spent time with them at weekly one-to-one meetings planning their work. I cut out any emotional side and simply asked them to look at what they needed to do to achieve the results I needed to see. We then worked out what steps they needed to take to achieve their targets, and then considered how I or the team could help them.

I was really happy to see that my audit junior took to this training like a duck to water. He'd just never worked that way before, but once he started, he powered through his work and eventually gained himself a great reputation.

But you win some, you lose some. The junior in the most recent case was not able to follow through on the plan. He simply didn't enjoy working to a schedule. He still kept making promises that he couldn't keep. He still didn't communicate any problems until after it was too late. I did manage to review his workload and free up other team members to help him, but when I left he was still not much better off than when I'd joined.

As for me, I used all the tips I'm sharing below, so yes, I have been overwhelmed, but I had a plan and it helped me to cope.

I also found that meditation (or mindfulness as it's being called now) really helps me. We'll talk more about that later, but I would like to make one point now. For those of you who don't buy into the whole 'happy clappy' image that meditation might conjure up, try thinking about it in another way. Meditation starts by focusing on breathing deeply. This ensures you get a good supply of oxygen into your body, which helps your body work more efficiently, more smoothly – the oxygen feeds your body what it needs – and this makes you feel better physically. Even if you ignore the emotional release, this physical release alone is worth just five minutes of your time a day. Who knows how much stress or medication you'll avoid in the long-run?

Actions – Don't Let it Overwhelm You

If you are constantly fire-fighting, then you need to stop and take stock. There has to be a better way – and you can find it.

Less overwhelm, more focus

You may have heard of the 80:20 rule – you can apply it to a lot of things. In this scenario, the theory is that eighty per cent of our workload contributes to twenty per cent of its value. That means only twenty per cent of our workload contributes a whopping eighty per cent of value. So what you need to do is identify the tasks that are most productive: the twenty per cent workload that yields eighty per cent value. Get that done first and you'll have achieved loads. Plus you'll be working more efficiently and saving yourself a lot of time and aggravation. You can then choose the most productive twenty per cent of the remaining work and complete that.

Less overwhelm, less stuff

Another reason we tend to feel overwhelmed is the sheer volume of 'stuff'. And by that I mean everything – emails, information, alternatives, choices, decisions. It's easy to get bogged down by all that noise and forget what it is we really need or want.

Something I do on a regular basis (about once every six months) is an email cull. I go through my emails and unsubscribe from anything I don't need. I might have seen one interesting article and had to part with my email address to get it, but actually I don't need their weekly newsletters clogging up my inbox.

We're in the golden age of information – if you want something later, you can always Google it. And when you have less unnecessary information coming through, it's easier to see what you really want to see, and you feel less overwhelmed by all those things you think you 'should' read (and we all know that isn't helpful).

Less overwhelm, less stress

The definition of overwhelm goes something like 'upset, overthrow, bury or drown beneath a huge mass of something/overpower in thought and feeling'.

So basically, the more overwhelmed you become, the more stressed you get. When you get stressed, your ability to focus deteriorates. When that happens, you spend lots of time doing a little bit of work that isn't helping you. Then you feel more overwhelmed at everything you need to get done that you're not getting done, which makes you feel stressed...a classic vicious circle.

It has to make sense to cut out the unnecessary garbage, by reducing whatever is cluttering your inbox, your to-do list and your headspace. This will unclutter your thoughts, restore your focus and thereby reduce your stress, leaving you free to get more done, which makes you feel better...a classic virtuous circle.

Tips – Taking Control

If something is unmanageable, then the first task is to chop it down and turn it into manageable chunks.

Tip 1 – Write it down

I am an inveterate list-maker, and it is particularly helpful when you are suffering from overwhelm. One of the things that happens when you get overwhelmed, whether it's at work or at home, or juggling both, is that you start to think about everything that you need to do. Then you start doing a little bit of everything and end up getting nowhere fast. So first of all – STOP. Take five minutes and do some deep breathing (see Item 7).

Once you're feeling calmer, start a list with two columns. Write down a list of all the things you have to get done. Then, in the second column write down the date/time that each task needs to be completed. Once this is sorted, you can start to prioritise.

Start with the things that are urgent, and the things that are important. Sometimes you'll have urgent things that aren't important but still need to be done. Sometimes you have important tasks that aren't urgent, so they keep getting left. There's a great little matrix that helps with this. Sort the points from your list into the matrix below.

Box 1	Box 2
URGENT and IMPORTANT	IMPORTANT but not urgent
Do now	Plan to do after all box 1 items and any immediate box 3 items
Box 3	Box 4
URGENT but not important	Not important or urgent
Do after box 1 activities, or delegate	Delegate or delete this item, or complete after all other tasks

Review your list daily, crossing things off (very satisfying) and amending the status as things change. The idea is that you gain some control, you can see where there are any potential bottlenecks, and you can ask for help in advance. For example, say at work you see that you have urgent and important tasks that will take a couple of days, but you need to get them all done in one day.

You now have something you can take to your manager to demonstrate the issue. You're also demonstrating that you are trying to solve the problem but it might take more manpower – something only your manager can help with. Or they may review the list and advise that some deadlines can be changed. Either way, you now have knowledge and therefore more control. This in turn makes you feel calmer, so you're actually more able to cope.

Another technique I use is putting everything in my Microsoft Outlook Calendar. I colour-code activities depending on their urgency and importance, and I block out the time I think each task is going to take. I review that each evening before I finish, so I know what I have planned for the next day. Then when I start in the morning I know what the plan is. It also helps me if plans change unexpectedly, because I can see what I can move and what needs to stay.

Again, it gives me greater information, clarity and control, so I feel better. Even if I have a lot to do, it stops me feeling overwhelmed because I have a plan and I just need to work through it. (And yes, I know it's a bit OTT, but I like lists and colour-coding stuff ...).

Tip 2 – Break it down

Picture this – you have a huge amount of work to get through, so much it's never-ending. You have no idea how or where to start, so you play around at the edges, not achieving much and not moving forward. That makes you feel overwhelmed and frustrated, which might make you feel you're not capable, when actually you're the perfect person for the job.

Instead of just diving in, think of your work day as an end product made up of building blocks. The first step is to identify how many blocks you have and how big those blocks are. Then work out which blocks make up the foundation, which are the next level, and so on until you get to the last building block. Once you've done that, you may want to take the first block, look at it in more detail and break it down a little more. By doing this, you'll find you've written yourself a project plan and you can start to work from there. It's still a big ask, but now you know how to start, how to progress and how to finish.

You also know where you are at any given time, so if something else is thrown into the mix, you know what can move and what can't. Again, you also have something tangible to take to your manager if you genuinely think there is too much for you to do in the time you have available.

Tip 3 – Block it out

Manage email interruption. We all know what it's like. You get thirty or forty emails a day ('Pffft, is that all?' I can hear some of you saying). Each time your computer pings* (* insert whatever noise yours makes here!), you have a quick look at the incoming mail and decide whether you can come back to it later or whether it needs attention now. But that also makes thirty or forty small interruptions in your day, leaving you working in something like ten-minute bursts.

Instead, have at least one or two chunks of time during your work day where you turn off email notifications, turn your phone to silent and ask colleagues not to interrupt you, if possible.

You can then spend that chunk of time concentrating on getting through your work. You could also allocate specific times of the day to check and action email – for example, first thing in the morning, before and after lunch, and last thing before you leave. You're still keeping up to date and on top of everything but you're managing that steady stream of distraction from the job in hand.

Item 7 – Coping Mindfully

'Do not dwell on the past, do not dream of the future, concentrate the mind on the present moment.'

Buddha (c. 563–483), Sage, philosopher and spiritual teacher and the man on whose teaching Buddhism is based

The whole 'overwhelm' thing actually leads me nicely on to breathing, and I mean that both in the literal sense of breaths in and out of your body, and also in the sense of your life breath and how that flows. Let me explain.

Most people, most of the time, take short, shallow breaths. When we panic (for example, when we're getting overwhelmed and finding it all too much to cope with) we take even shallower breaths. It's just the way our bodies and brains are wired up. Shallow breathing is enough to keep us functioning but it doesn't really go 'all the way'.

Deep breathing, on the other hand, will work miracles for you. It will decrease your stress levels, it will positively impact on your hormone levels and overall it will boost your general feel-good factor. With such a wide array of benefits on offer it's worth making time for deep breathing for just five minutes a day.

Just breathe

It's not difficult. Stop everything and focus on your breathing, starting at the beginning of a breath and following it all the way through. Inhale slowly and gently through your nose, taking the breath deep inside your body. Notice that tiny pause just before you gently, slowly and deliberately exhale completely. Be aware of the breath leaving your body, then notice again that tiny infinitesimal pause before you repeat the whole process again. And that's it. Just keep it going for five minutes.

Once you have done your five minutes a day, you can go back to twenty-three hours and fifty-five minutes of shallow, 'this'll do for now' breathing. But each day after that, try for a little more deep breathing and a little less shallow breathing.

I think the way we live our lives is becoming more and more like the short, shallow breaths we all take most of the time. Life, for most of us, no matter where we are, is fast-paced; we're inundated with communication, with information, with demands on our time, attention and emotions.

We spend our time doing one thing while worrying about another, and stressing about when we'll have time to get round to doing a third. We're continually fretting over what we did or didn't do well in the past and we're anxious about the future, to the point where we're probably not doing that great a job in the present.

Stop and smell the roses

As Ferris Bueller (number 15 in *Empire* magazine's 100 Greatest Movie Characters) said so memorably in the 1980s' classic teen coming-of-age film *Ferris Bueller's Day Off*: 'Life moves pretty fast. If you don't stop and look around once in a while, you could miss it.' That's what I mean about life breath. I couldn't express it any better than Ferris. Life moves really fast. We move with it – we have to – but we don't always stop to smell the roses.

I used to get really annoyed with my dog when I took him out for his walks. I used to try to combine his walks with getting my own exercise. That's one of the reasons having a dog is so great, right? Except my dog doesn't really do well-paced walks. For three seconds he sprints, then all of a sudden he'll slow down and have a good sniff at something interesting or pungent. Sometimes he stops completely so he can enjoy sniffing the flowers as we walk past a particularly fragrant garden. Even when he's done, he'll just stand there, contemplating the air.

I would get really annoyed that we were losing time and I wasn't getting the exercise I needed. I'd tug on his lead and chivvy him along. He'd sprint again for five seconds, then slow down yet again. Perhaps someone would stop us and have a play with him (he's a people dog, and ridiculously cute – everyone says so, it's not just my opinion). Walking the dog became another stressful thing for me to do. It always took longer than I thought and I wasn't getting my exercise.

Then one day, it just struck me. The dog wasn't doing anything wrong; this was his outside time and he was simply enjoying it. He was literally taking time to smell the roses. I was the one trying to rush us through this activity so I could get on with the next one. I wasn't paying attention to him, to the roses or the trees. I definitely didn't want to stay and chat to strangers even if they had time or it was only ten seconds. I was walking the dog in shallow breathing mode.

As soon as I realised what I was doing, I stopped using our walks as part of my exercise routine, so now our walks are just that – our walks.

Now, when I pick up his lead, I don't worry about how quickly I can get us around the block. I don't take my watch or phone, we just head out. If he's in an energetic mood, we can be back in a half hour, if not, we mooch along and it takes longer. A few times we've got back home and wanted to stay out, so have headed in a different direction. And on our walks I notice what he's sniffing, I check out the same gardens and flowers he does. And I enjoy the random chats with people who just want to stroke my lovely, smiley, friendly puppy. I practise my deep breathing on our walks, too, making the most of the fresh air. I feel as though I connect with the earth and with my pooch. Everything is on pause for that time every day, and it makes life flow a bit better.

It's like that at work too. I didn't notice the good times: the great things I'd learned, the fantastic skills I was picking up, the friends I'd made who are still here now. While it was actually happening, I was oblivious.

When I look at back at what I was like in my very first job (a three-week contract helping to clear some filing), I shake my head at myself. I had no idea what I was doing. It was the first time I'd worked in an office and I thought it would be like college and university – lots of bright minds, fun and joking around but with nicer clothes and shiny new stationery. It was not. It was three weeks of filing for seven hours a day with a sad little cheese sandwich at lunchtimes to break up the monotony. In my very first 'proper' accounting job, I still had no idea. I thought everyone was my friend and had my best interests at heart. I didn't know I'd been labelled 'Purchase Ledger Clerk number two' and that was supposed to be that. When I realised what had happened I was miserable. I used to get depressed wondering if this was all there was to life – this series of panicked days and sleepless nights when I was always busy, always trying to catch up, always shallow breathing.

Enjoy the moment

That's what I mean about breathing. You might wonder why I'm even talking about this. I guess it's because we spend so long at the office. Look at the proportion of time you spend at work – you probably see some of your work colleagues more than you see your family and friends. And yes, you're there to work and you're getting paid to deliver something. But you're also investing a little bit of you, however small, into that space, that environment, those people. Look at the amount of years – decades in fact – you'll be at work. It's important that it doesn't become a place that sucks the soul and the joy out of you. And it's up to you to find a way to make sure that doesn't happen.

At work, we're always busy looking at the next step, or focusing on what we haven't done, or what we might get caught out on. Sometimes you just need to let life flow at its own pace. It may sometimes feel as though other people are getting more done than you; there may be things you have to put off – but how important is it, really? None of that even comes close to the feel-good factor you get from just enjoying being where you are, doing what you're doing. So if you can, just for five minutes a day, try to breathe life in a bit more deeply.

If you're at the start of your working life, enjoy the excitement, the thrill of learning, growing, improving, changing. If you've been there a while, look back and notice how far you've come, the skills you've gained, the contacts you've made, how much better you are at what you do today than you were when you first started out.

I'm genuinely amazed when I look back over my career to date at some of the things I find so easy now, that I either never even imagined I'd be doing (like leading a team of forty people), or that I found some unexpected joy in (like coaching someone and watching them start to believe in themselves, in their own potential).

Look at what it is about this job, this office, this environment that gives you a buzz, a spark, that fires you up a bit. If the spark has died down or even out, then work out how you can rekindle it. Take a breath, a proper, deep breath.

Actions – Mindfulness

A great way to slow it all down and focus on you and your joy again is to practise mindfulness.

More mindfulness, better focus

The first thing you learn to do when you practice mindfulness is the art of focusing. You're focusing on your in-breaths and out-breaths for a concentrated amount of time. This actually helps your brain use the same technique in other situations as well, like at the office. And the longer your mindfulness sessions last, the more practice you're getting at improving your focus, which benefits you in other aspects of your life too.

More mindfulness, less anxiety

When you meditate, you weaken a particular neural connection in your brain that creates and enhances your stress reactors. This is good because it means when something happens that would normally cause you a lot of stress, mindfulness helps reduce the level of stress you experience. That means you can look at the situation more rationally and react in a more appropriate way. So you won't have a melt-down if someone hasn't filled the photocopier paper tray.

More mindfulness, better memory

Researchers have found that people who practise mindfulness are able to adjust the brainwave that screens out distractions and increases productivity more quickly than those who don't practise mindfulness. And this ability to ignore distractions might explain the increased ability to remember new facts – very helpful when learning your presentation.

Tips – Restoring Your Deep Breathing

Take measures to help make mindfulness work for you.

Tip 1 – Start small

Initially, just aim for five minutes a day, ideally at the start or end of the day. Build it up to five minutes twice a day and then longer for each session, if you find that useful. The fact that you're doing something, however small, on a regular basis, will help your body release the stresses and strains it's holding on to, and help you clear your mind.

Tip 2 – Focus on your breathing

There are lots of different ways to practise mindfulness, but the easiest way I've found is to simply focus on your breath. Once you're sitting comfortably, concentrate on breathing in through your nose to a count of two or three (whichever is most comfortable for you). Follow the breath as it moves through your body. Notice that infinitesimal pause at the end. Then follow it leaving your body as you breathe out through your mouth for the same count. Again, notice that miniscule pause right at the end, before you do it all again. Do this for five minutes a day to start with. Focusing just on the breath clears your mind, and the deep breathing helps your body get the oxygen it needs. You'll feel great afterwards.

Tip 3 – Get your prep right

It sounds obvious but it's easy to forget that you need to make sure you're in an environment where you won't be disturbed. Turn off your phone and any other devices. Maybe put some relaxing music on in the background if it helps. Other than that, don't worry about trying to turn your mindfulness space into a sanctuary, just go for it and enjoy the calm. And although a serene space is ideal, you can actually use this technique anywhere. I've even done it in my car in the office car park at lunchtime (ooer!) when I've needed to get some calm back into my day.

Item 8 – Coping with Crappy Days

'Be still, sad heart! And cease repining. Behind clouds is the sun still shining; Thy fate is the common fate of all, into each life some rain must fall.'

Henry Wadsworth Longfellow (1807–1882), American poet and educator

I'm a great believer in thinking positively, as you might have sussed. I think you attract more of what you think about, so if you are thinking about what you want in life, you are more likely to get it. Even if you don't believe in any form of attraction thinking, it's still a great idea to focus on what you want – it keeps it sharp, it reminds you why you're doing what you're doing and it spurs you on when things get tough.

But I get seriously annoyed with people who espouse the theory that you have to be happy, positive and full of sunshine all the time. You know the ones. Woe-betide you if you're having an off day. Just think yourself happy...go on, do it now!

Rubbish.

First of all, it's just not practical or realistic to spend 365 days of the year, 24 hours a day in that state. Of course you want to be positive as much as possible, but as the quote above states so eloquently – into each life some rain must fall. (Those of us living in the UK are lucky enough to enjoy a lot of rain.)

Second – think about it in a different way. If you were happy all day, every day – where's the variety? Where's your rainbow? If you're on one tempo all the time how do you even know what that tempo is? Again, it's clichéd because it's true; you need a little rain for a rainbow.

So you had a bad day

We all have days where we're a bit grumpy, or things haven't gone our way. The tech-gremlins may be waging war on your gadgets, the kids playing up, your boss/team/colleagues being especially difficult or obtuse, perhaps your hairdryer blew up, or your water tank is leaking. (That last one happened to me the morning of an important presentation at work and the day before I was due to fly out on holiday.) The list is endless and irritating. But these things happen. Pretending they won't happen, or aren't happening or that it's all okay when they happen isn't necessarily helpful.

Bottling up frustration isn't helpful either. Plastering a smile over your frown probably isn't going to make you feel better – and you'll look really odd. What's more helpful is to recognise this is all part of life's ebb and flow, and know that it sucks but it'll pass. You are allowed to be annoyed or grumpy or irritated when something annoying or grumpy-making or irritating happens. That's an acceptable reaction. When life ebbs rather than flows or hits you with a low blow, you will feel bad so just let your negative emotions out.

I remember very clearly, when I was first diagnosed with cancer, my employers offered me some free counselling with a trained therapist to help me cope. During one of our conversations I was ranting at how unfair it was that I had to deal with this horrible thing. I said I wished I was still in my oblivious perfect world and she asked if I could see an upside. The silver lining was that at least now I knew life wasn't all a bed of roses, and coping with this illness meant I could cope with anything life threw at me. At the time I couldn't understand why anyone would think like that. Why would I want to be looking for the silver lining? That meant I had to see past the clouds but I wasn't ready to do that. I just wanted the clouds never to have existed.

But if I ever met her again, I would tell her that conversation has stayed with me ever since. I'd tell her I'm grateful to her for showing me that actually we all have clouds to deal with – of different shapes, sizes and intensity, of course – and it's how we cope that helps us develop.

At a recent contract, I worked with a girl who took an instant dislike to me. She was a manager who was part of my team and was supposed to report to me, but would cancel meetings, ignore my emails, and try and undermine me in any way she could. Plus her work was unreliable because she picked and chose what she delivered on. I couldn't work out why she was behaving as she did.

I like to think I'm a fairly supportive manager. Yes, I expect my teams to deliver the goods, but I genuinely care that they don't burn themselves out in the process, that they do something they enjoy and that we have some fun. I knew she was overworked and I tried to understand her workload so I could help, but she was having none of it. She would fluctuate between telling me all her problems (whilst reciting her CV to me), telling me she was too busy to talk (whilst reciting her CV to me) or ignoring me completely (probably whilst reciting her CV to herself).

Find your safety valve

It came to a point at which she was seriously affecting the way the team worked – not to mention the way I worked, and also my boss. And it didn't help that he didn't like her much anyway. I couldn't let things continue as they were so I decided I needed to put an end to this behaviour. I spoke to HR just to make sure I was approaching things in the best way possible.

And it was then that I found out she had expected to be given my role. And looking at her CV I saw that she'd been made redundant a couple of times before she got her current position. Knowing I was dealing with someone who was probably very insecure about their own capabilities whilst believing they had been passed over for promotion made it much easier for me to find a way to work with her.

I had a serious discussion with her at which I told her what I expected from anyone working for me – I felt she needed to hear it, so she was very clear that no matter what had gone on in the past and whatever her expectations were now, this was the current status quo. Once I'd got that difficult conversation out of the way I could take a look at her workload and how best I could support her, something her previous manager hadn't done.

It still wasn't the best working relationship, but it was better. And if she was having a really bad day and really annoying me, I went in to my boss' office, shut the door and asked him if I could have a five minute off-the-record rant (and, of course, I returned the favour at other times).

So work out how best you deal with things – do you need to rant? Then find a friend who will let you rant. Do you need someone to help you see beyond the crap? Then find someone who will do that for you. Do you need to hide away for a while? Then go and do that.

Depending on what's annoying me, I will either rant with one of my inner circle, knowing it will go no further, or I'll take myself out of the equation.

I've found that time and distance from a situation are both great healers. I'll burrow down into the sofa, with the pooch for company, and a good book or film, enjoy a long snooze and ride the storm out.

When things have settled a bit, I'll put my head above the parapet and work out how I restore the situation to normal.

One of my brothers takes himself off for a run or hits the crap out of his punch bag – as he points out, he's releasing his frustration and getting a great workout!

And then, when things are clear again, I genuinely do find I appreciate things a bit more. I'm grateful for the storm and I'm grateful for the sun afterwards. Ebb and flow, clouds and sun, rain and rainbows. It's the combination that makes life interesting.

Actions – Sleep

One of the first things to be disrupted when we're feeling low or stressed is our sleep. And we often under estimate what a huge impact sleep has on us. We think we can get by on almost none, but that's just not the case.

Sleep more, learn better

A research study published in *Science* magazine (6 June 2014: 1173–11789) looked at the link between better sleep and better learning, examining in detail the underlying ways in which sleep helps the brain form and store memories.

'We've known for a long time that sleep plays an important role in learning and memory,' said senior investigator Wen-Biao Gan, a professor at the Skirball Institute. 'If you don't sleep well, you don't learn well.'

The scientists involved in the study tracked real-time changes in mouse memory during sleep and wakefulness. Fifteen mice were trained for one hour to walk forwards and backwards on top of a rotating rod. Then, some mice were allowed to sleep for seven hours, whilst the others were kept awake.

The team noticed that the brains of the mice that were allowed to snooze formed significantly more connections between neurons than those of the mice that were not allowed to sleep. This indicated that learning and memory formation occurred more easily and effectively after sleep.

Some of the sleeping mice had their sleep deliberately disrupted. They performed less well than the mice who were allowed to sleep through continuously.

This indicates memory formation occurs overwhelmingly during deep or slow-wave sleep, the phase where the brain rehashes that day's goings on. Scientists also noted physical changes in the brain during this stage of deep sleep – in which dendritic spine growth (dendritic spines are tiny offshoots which grow from neuron branches) occurs, with the new dendrites connecting with other neurons to pass information on that helps build an inventory of memories. The sleep-deprived mice sprouted far fewer dendritic spines.

'Finding out sleep promotes new connections between neurons is new. Nobody knew this before,' said Wen-Biao Gan.

Sleep more, fight ageing

Sleep decreases stress hormones, like cortisol. Lack of sleep makes cortisol levels rise. Cortisol inhibits the formation of collagen, a protein that works a bit like 'glue that holds the body together'. That's why sleep deprivation can actually accelerate ageing – yet another reason to get a good seven hours each night!

Sleep more, weigh less

Medical evidence is throwing up some interesting links between sleep and weight. Scientists believe the quantity and possibly the quality of your sleep are linked to a host of hormonal activity that's then also tied to your appetite.

'One of the more interesting ideas that is now gaining momentum is the appreciation of the fact that sleep and sleep disruption do remarkable things to the body – including possibly influencing our weight,' says David Rapoport, MD, associate professor and director of the Sleep Medicine Program at the New York University School of Medicine in New York City.

Doctors have always been aware that many hormones are affected by sleep, but Rapoport says it wasn't until recently that appetite entered the picture. He says this came about through research on the hormones leptin and ghrelin. Doctors say that both can influence our appetite, and studies show that production of both may be influenced by how much or how little we sleep.

If you've ever had one of those nights where you just couldn't sleep and then a day when no amount of food made you feel full no matter how many times you raided the vending machine at work, then you've experienced the effects of lack of sleep on the leptin and ghrelin hormones. So, getting a good night's sleep will leave you more than just refreshed, it'll help you fight the hunger pangs, too.

Tips – Improving Your Sleep Patterns

Try to make sure that you are getting enough good-quality sleep.

Tip 1 – Regulate

If you can, try to keep to same bedtime and waking up time, even at the weekend. It helps to regulate your body clock, so your body recognises when it should be winding down, and ultimately this could help you fall asleep and stay asleep for most of the night.

Tip 2 – Routine

Find your own relaxing bedtime routine. The idea is to start to prepare your body for a wind-down to sleep. So working right up until 10.30pm, then expecting to fall asleep straight away isn't advisable. Instead, at least an hour or two before bed, stop doing anything stressful and/or strenuous.

Take a bath, make a warm drink (no caffeine obviously) and read a good book, or listen to some chilled out, relaxing music. Whatever it is that makes you feel more relaxed is perfect. The idea is to work with your circadian rhythms (your body's internal natural pre-programmed rhythms/clock) so your body understands bedtime and sleep are next on the list.

Tip 3 – Get sleep-ready

Make sure your bedroom is a little cooler than the rest of the house. Avoid bright lights in the bedroom at bedtime too (bright lights trick your body into thinking it is still daytime and this kick starts your body into waking mode again). Think about investing in blackout blinds if your curtains let in too much light – this stops you waking earlier than planned during the summer. If you can't afford blackout blinds, then an eye mask (not the gloopy, beauty salon kind, but the ones you get as freebies on night flights) might be worth a try instead.

Bright lights also include things like the lights from laptops, tablets and TVs, so if at all possible, keep these in a different room so they don't mess with your sleep. I used to read on my tablet at night regularly, and end up awake until 4am. When I started leaving the tablet downstairs and switched to good old fashioned paper books at bedtime I nodded off much faster.

Think about the sounds that help or don't help you sleep. If you need absolute silence, then get some heavy-duty ear plugs. Maybe a gentle sleep CD with comforting sounds will help you drift off.

Keep a pad of paper and a pen near your bed. If you have any thoughts keeping you up, write them all down on the pad – it'll help to stop them running rings inside your head, so you can focus on getting to sleep. And if you're having one of those nights where you're really struggling to get to sleep and just can't sleep, then don't keep trying. Get up, go into another room and do something relaxing until you feel tired. Then try going back to bed.

Item 9 – Coping with Change

'Nothing lasts forever, so live it up; drink it down, laugh it off, avoid the bullshit. Take chances and never have regrets because, at one point, everything you did was exactly what you wanted.'

Marilyn Monroe (1926–1962), American actress, model and singer

Once I had got the idea of being in the flow and coping with the ups and downs, the next big whammy for me was the realization that nothing is for ever. Just as I had settled into the university lifestyle, I graduated and was back home. The minute I got used to being a trainee accountant and found myself an awesome bunch of friends, they started moving on to their next jobs. When I got used to working with one boss, she moved and I got another one and had to start all over again.

Working in audit helped to train me to cope with change – because as an auditor you get used to meeting new businesses and new people every other week. You get used to doing things one way and then having to learn to do them another way to match your clients' systems. That gave me quite a lot of experience of coping with change and I think I'm okay at it (not great maybe, but not bad). But along the way I've seen how the inability to cope with change has affected some of my family, friends and work colleagues.

Fear of change

When I first told my dad I was moving out in a few months, he didn't speak to me for two months. He couldn't cope with the idea that I was not doing what all Indian girls my age did: move straight from their father's home to their husband's home. It upset his ideas, his values and the way he saw me and himself. It took a good talking to from some of his more open-minded friends to see that this was a good thing.

Now, almost fifteen years later, he loves the fact that I'm independent, reliant on no-one but me, and happy. But that change was really painful for him.

One woman I was managing at work a while ago couldn't cope with the idea of having to tell me in advance what overtime she would be doing. She'd been used to doing what she wanted and just having it signed off.

When I came in and changed things she couldn't cope. We had tears (hers), tantrums (hers) and a lot of pain (hers, mine and the team). In the end, she refused to do any overtime. I duly distributed that work amongst the rest of the team, which actually hurt her more in the long-term as she then lost out on the additional pay.

A few weeks later she came to me ahead of time with details of why she needed to be working late and what she would achieve, asking me to sign off on it, which I did, happily. After that, the problem disappeared.

She was over-reacting, but for a completely understandable reason; ultimately it was born out of fear. Fear that her steady world would crumble. It was the same for my dad – his reluctance stemmed from fear of the unknown. What would people think? How would I cope alone? What would this mean for my marriage prospects (to be honest, I think it's my personality that might affect those more, but hey ho!)?

Confront the fear

I completely understand that fear. But the fear won't stop the change happening. It didn't in either of those examples. Change is the one certainty. Life is all about flow and it never stops flowing. So if change is going to happen, whether we like it or not, the only thing we have any control over is how we choose to react to that change. Will we embrace it willingly, openly and yes, possibly slightly warily, but with our heads held high?

Or will we rage against the tide, will we need to be dragged along kicking and screaming, and use all our energy in fighting the inevitable? Either choice is valid because it's your choice to make. But one leaves you completely exhausted and frustrated.

The other choice? I can only tell you how it is for me – and for me, it's great. I like the fact that things won't always be the same. If things are tough I know that won't last forever. If things are good, I appreciate them more, knowing that won't last forever either. Life is always interesting and infinitely more exciting.

Initiate change and take control

But it isn't enough anymore. What I love even more than accepting change is initiating change. Things are going to change anyway, right? So why not make some of the changes yourself – take a little more control?

You can do it in any number of different ways. One way for me is contracting. It means I'm forced into new situations every few months. It keeps the money coming in, sure, but it also means I never get comfortable in an environment that I know isn't in my long-term plans.

I also choose to start new projects. I control change in that if those projects don't work, I put my hand up, accept that it hasn't gone the way I'd have liked and I move on. I learn what I can, but I don't see anything as a failure any more. For a while I ran my own NLP practice and I loved helping my clients. But I found the work wasn't quite the right fit for me so I accepted I needed a change and went into contracting.

Maybe one day I'll go back and do some coaching because I loved that part of the therapy work, and I have loved coaching my teams through the years.

I also started an online jewellery store while I was between contracts because I suddenly got the idea into my head and had time to try it out. I enjoyed the buzz of being able to source great pieces of jewellery and share them with the world. And I loved the buzz of someone buying something I'd chosen and then telling me how much they loved it. While it was a lot of fun, it didn't fulfil me, so I moved on, but both of those projects have given me some great experiences and useful skills. (And one of them has given me a lovely collection of jewellery too!)

If you look at all the most successful people at work – those you aspire to emulate – they don't fight change, they don't even just adapt to change, they actively choose it.

Richard Branson comes to mind as a great example because that is one of the traits that make him so successful. He's always been focused on what he wants, on his personal goals, and found a way to align them with the goals of his various businesses. He has always actively sought change, tried new things. Sometimes they've been phenomenally successful and sometimes not. Regardless, he continues to experiment, change and grow. It's an attitude I really admire.

Looking at the example of Branson and other successful people also illustrates the importance of being honest with yourself when things aren't going well, and being brave about dealing with that. Successful people review and learn, then they change.

I started a contract recently that I wasn't sure about. Within the first few days I knew it wasn't for me but I felt that it was too soon to throw in the towel. About a month later, things hadn't improved and I could see that they were about to get a lot worse because I recognised the signs from something I'd seen in a previous contract. I decided that rather than go with a change I knew I would be unhappy with, I would leave. I chose that, even though it meant I would be out of a job and out of funds. Despite that, I knew I'd be okay. Change doesn't always go the way you think it will, but that's not a good enough reason to avoid it.

So for me, accepting and sometimes initiating change is exhilarating, liberating, a bit scary and really exciting.

Actions – Gratitude

I know, I know – the number crunchers, lawyers and sceptics amongst you are having a mini-seizure just at the word 'gratitude'. But hear me out – the tips I've included are in here because they work.

So why gratitude? And how does it help you cope with change? We tend to resist change because of fear – of losing control, of the unknown, or all sorts of other reasons. Gratitude techniques help manage that fear by focusing on the beneficial aspects of a situation, and combating and reducing the negative feelings that aren't helping us.

The art and habit of gratitude is just starting to get the acknowledgment it deserves. More and more studies are being done showing the link between practising the attitude of gratitude and a whole host of benefits (three of which we list below) – and, what's more, it's absolutely free.

In addition, you don't pay anyone to do it for you or with you, you don't need any special tools or equipment, it doesn't take long and it makes you feel awesome. Surely it's worth reading three little tips?

Feel grateful, stress less

Did you know that gratitude helps you to cope with stress better? Scientists are starting to see links between an attitude of gratitude and the ability to cope better with everyday stresses and strains. Stress is generally a feeling brought on and exacerbated by our negative thoughts. Gratitude techniques focus our mind on the positives, which tend to make us feel calmer and happier, thus reducing the feeling of stress. Practising gratitude techniques daily is a bit like a workout for your brain – you are training your positive-thinking muscles to kick in more often and to be stronger than the negative-thinking muscles that lead to stress.

Feel grateful, sleep better

I know – I was surprised, too. But it's true. We all know from the previous chapter that good, restful sleep is essential. And we've all had those sleepless nights that have left us exhausted so we end up going through the next day feeling like a zombie.

Sleep is affected by stress. Practising gratitude reduces that stress. This can increase our sleep quality, reduce the time it takes us to get to sleep in the first place and help us sleep for longer. And a good night's sleep will also help you cope better with your Horroffice. All this for a measly five minutes of thinking about good stuff that's happened to you – a pretty good deal if you ask me.

Feel grateful, exercise more

This is another benefit of gratitude that I was not expecting. An American study that lasted 11 weeks found that people who used a weekly gratitude journal exercised an extra forty minutes per week compared to the control group, who didn't use a journal. I guess if you feel grateful for having a healthy body you might just work a bit harder at keeping it healthy.

Then you'll feel even more grateful for being fit and healthy. Which makes you work harder to stay that way...you get it! Being fit and healthy also means less time off sick from work, as well as feeling better while you're there. (Plus your suits will fit better!) All this, and it was based on a weekly journal – imagine the benefits if you practise gratitude daily.

Tips – Cultivating a State of Mind

Find some ways to incorporate the practice of gratitude into your day so that it suits your lifestyle and schedule.

Tip 1 – Speak the language

People who practise the art of gratitude use a very different language from most people. They talk about benefits, blessings, luck, abundance, gifts, giving, being fortunate, being thankful and so on. Try it out for yourself. When talking, make a conscious effort to avoid negative language and embrace more positive words – notice how it makes you feel.

Tip 2 – Use a gratitude journal

Set aside five minutes at the end of each day to think of at least three things you're grateful for – it might be nabbing that sweet parking spot at the front of the office, it might be your partner cooking dinner for you, or just a stranger smiling at you. If you look back over your day, you'll find at least three things to be grateful for. Write this down in your journal. When you're feeling low, go back over your journal and have a read through. It'll help you pick your mood up again. This daily process also helps your brain get into a gratitude mindset.

Tip 3 – Act it out

Start to say thank you, or to smile at people more often. Try and do one random nice thing for someone each day – it might be as small as doing a tea round at work, offering to pet-sit for a friend, or sending a text to let your mum to let her know you're thinking of her. Just do something every single day. It is the act of doing something positive that triggers the feelings of gratitude in you because it is the person doing the favour that feels the most benefit. If you do something positive for someone else, you get the biggest 'feel-good' factor from it. So, it's really worthwhile giving a little something to someone even if it's for no other reason than to feel good.

Item 10 – Beyond Coping

'Whatever you decide to do, make sure it makes you happy.'

Paulo Coelho (b.1947), Brazilian lyricist and novelist

Ultimately, I honestly believe the only reason you should do anything is because it makes you happy now or it's going to make you happy in the future. Exercising and eating healthily come in the second category for me – walking the dog or reading a great book come in the first. Both are still steps on my path to my happy.

Working at all the different offices I've experienced has also convinced me that a happy work environment makes for a much more productive work force. And that's what you need to think about. Are you happy at work right now? If not, what can you do to make it better? Because the better you feel at work, the better you'll perform at work. Which makes you feel better, and that makes you perform better – a virtuous circle.

That's it really. Not quite the sum of all my knowledge, but definitely the best and most relevant bits at the moment. I hope it has been useful.

If I had to summarise, it's all about you, but in a good way. Don't buy into other people's bullshit. Don't buy into their dreams either. It's all about you. Don't waste your time comparing yourself to them. It's all about you. Just compare yourself to yourself, and adjust accordingly. It's all about you. Don't bother chasing the money. Chase your joy and the money will come. *Your* joy. Why? Because it's all about you. But when you do get the money, don't throw it away. It's yours. You deserve it. Why? Because it's all about you. Fight – fight for your right to find and follow your joy. If you lose your way, just stop. Take a breath. A deep breath. Meditate. Get back to you. Find your flow. *Your* flow. And when you find your flow, go with it. It leads to your joy. When you find your joy, pause. Smell the roses. Savour your joy. Feel the flow. Don't expect your joy today to look like your joy yesterday. Know that it definitely won't look the same tomorrow. That's okay. Enjoy it in the now. I definitely am.

Action – Be Your Own Best Friend

There is only one action here and that is to be your own best friend.

It has so many benefits, though, that I have only been able to touch the tip of the iceberg in terms of describing what it can do for you.

Most people are their own worst critics. We all tend to judge ourselves far more harshly than we would anyone else.

Take a second to think about it. When something goes wrong, when you make a mistake, when you say something silly, what thoughts go through your head? Is it something along the lines of, 'Aargh, idiot! Why did I do that? I've completely messed up. No wonder my boss thinks I'm incompetent'. Or do you say, 'Just be cool. Why couldn't I just be cool – I sound like a nutter. He's never going to ask me out now. Yup – I'll be alone. For. EVER. Well played.'

Does any of that sound familiar? And yet, if it was your friend telling you they'd messed up at work, or on a date, or ruined the new cupboard they were trying to put together, would you say that to them? Of course not. You would reassure them that we all make mistakes, you would sympathise, you'd tell them it probably wasn't that bad and help them come up with a way to fix things, or to reconcile themselves to the situation.

So why don't we do that for ourselves? Why aren't we kinder to ourselves? And how does being so harsh help?

Sometimes it's a 'get in first' thing. If you say how stupid you are, no-one else can say it to you and make you feel worse.

Sometimes it's damage limitation – if you paint the worst picture, people might look at you and say, 'oh, it's not as bad as you think.' Both those things may be true but it's still not healthy. What's more, if it's a habit, then those harsh and negative thoughts are going around our heads all the time, bashing down our self-esteem. It doesn't sound like much fun to me.

So what if, as an experiment, instead of allowing all those negative thoughts to run wild, you start to corral them into a box in the corner of your mind, close and seal the box (use that strong industrial-strength brown tape from the post-room, so there's no chance of escape) and label the box 'Rubbish'. And then bin the box.

Instead of beating yourself up, why not try treating yourself the way you treat your closest friends and family: with kindness, encouragement and nurturing.

When you fall down, how about, instead of kicking yourself harder for having the temerity to fall, you check for scrapes, bandage them up, kiss them better, help yourself up again, and move on?

Just be your own best friend. Every time something happens, think to yourself: 'If this was my friend Ted, what would I say to him?' Then say those same words to yourself. Take care of yourself and do things that make you feel nurtured, cherished, and strong.

Watch those negative thoughts – if they start to get carried away again, get out the lasso and another box – you know the drill. Accept yourself – be kind to yourself – love yourself.

'I may not be who I ought to be,

I know I'm not all that I want to be,

But I've come a long way from who I used to be,

And I won't give up on becoming what I know I can be.'

Unknown

Item 11 – Any Other Business

Now we come to that bit of the meeting where you dump all the other stuff you couldn't fit into the main part. There a just a couple of extra things I wanted to share with you.

If you head to www.heenapattni.com you can grab a copy of my fabulous 'Ten Top Tips for Coping with the Horroffice' – print it out, stick it in your bag, pin it to your desk, stick it under your keyboard. That way you always have something to turn to if you're having 'one of those days'!

And just for fun, I've added one last lovely little tick list for you to enjoy! I've included actions you can take every day which will help you feel fabulous. Just tick off whichever ones tickle your fancy each day and enjoy!

Action	MON	TUE	WED	THU	FRI	SAT	SUN
Meditate (5 minutes)							
Read goals							
Visualise goals (5 minutes)							
Action goals (10 minutes)							
Dance like a loon (5 minutes)							
Laugh at stuff (3 times)							
Exercise (10 minutes)							
Gratitude stuff (5 minutes)							
Sleep (8 hours)							

Remember, you can download this tick list and the Ten Top Tips to Coping with the Horroffice cheat sheet at www.heenapattni.com.

www.ingramcontent.com/pod-product-compliance
Lightning Source LLC
Chambersburg PA
CBHW050512210326
41521CB00011B/2425